W.A.R. CRY

A Sound of Worship That Breaks Every Battle

By

Sherrell Attaway

This book is a work of nonfiction. Any references to individuals, events, or experiences are shared for inspirational and educational purposes. Names and identifying details may have been changed to protect privacy.

All Scripture quotations are taken from the King James Version (KJV) of the Bible.

Published by
Women of Purpose Publishers
For speaking engagements, ministry opportunities, or inquiries:
Email: pastorattaway@gmail.com

ISBN:
Printed in the United States of America

Dedication

This book is dedicated to God,
my Keeper, my Deliverer, and the One who taught me
how to fight in the Spirit and win in the natural.

To every warrior in the faith,
those who have cried in secret, battled in silence,
and stood firm when it felt like everything was falling apart,
this is for you.

To the ones who did not give up,
even when the warfare was heavy,
the attacks were relentless,
and the nights were long,
your cry did not go unheard.

I dedicate this to those who are learning
that your worship is not just a song,
it is a weapon.

To my family,
my husband, Damien Attaway,
my daughters, Damieona, Damiela, and Destiny,
and my grandchildren, Kyree, Khorey, and Charmani,
thank you for your love, your patience, and your unwavering
support.

To every intercessor, prayer warrior, and believer
who understands that some battles are not fought with hands,
but on your knees,
keep crying out.

Because every tear, every prayer, every sound of surrender
becomes a W.A.R. CRY that shakes heaven
and defeats the enemy.

This is for the fighters.
This is for the faithful.
This is for those who refuse to lose.

Sherrell Attaway

Table of Contents

A Prayer Before You Begin

Father,

Awaken the sound within me.

Break every layer of silence, fear, and pride
that has kept my voice bound.

Teach me how to worship You deeply,
adore You purely,
and reverence You fully.

And when the weight of life presses on me,
let a W.A.R. Cry rise out of my spirit
that heaven will respond to.

In Jesus' name, Amen.

What is a W.A.R. Cry?

W.A.R. – Worship • Adoration • Reverence

W – Worship

Worship is more than a song.
It is a lifestyle.

It is the posture of your heart fully surrendered to God.

When you worship, you acknowledge who God is.
Not just for what He does,
but for His holiness, His sovereignty, and His love.

John 4:24
"God is Spirit, and those who worship Him must worship in spirit
and in truth."

Worship shifts atmospheres.
Worship invites His presence.
Worship is your weapon.

A – Adoration

Adoration is deep love expressed toward God.

It is when your words, your heart, and your affection
are poured out toward Him.

Not asking.
Just loving.

Not requesting.
Just honoring.

Psalm 95:6
"Oh come, let us worship and bow down: let us kneel before the
Lord our maker."

Adoration says:

God, I love You for who You are.

R – Reverence

Reverence is holy respect and honor for God.

It is recognizing His power, His authority, and His majesty.

It keeps you humble.
It keeps you aligned.
It keeps you aware that He is God and we are not.

Hebrews 12:28
"Let us have grace, whereby we may serve God acceptably with
reverence and godly fear."

Reverence protects your relationship with God.

Declaration

I will not remain silent.
I will not suppress what God placed inside of me.

I will worship with my whole heart.
I will adore Him without condition.
I will reverence Him with my life.

My sound will rise.
My spirit will respond.
And heaven will answer.

Introduction
The Sound That Heaven Responds To

There is a sound.

Not produced by instruments.
Not taught in rehearsal.
Not learned through church tradition.

It is a sound that comes from deep within the soul.

A sound birthed in pressure.
Formed in pain.
Released in surrender.

This sound is called a W.A.R. Cry.

Many know how to shout.
Few know how to cry in the Spirit.

Because a real cry is not performance.

It is position.

It is the place where Worship, Adoration, and Reverence collide with desperation and produce a sound that heaven cannot ignore.

Throughout Scripture, every time a true cry was released, God responded.

Not because of perfection.

But because of posture.

He responds to surrender.
He responds to desperation.
He responds to authenticity.

This book is not just meant to be read.

It is meant to awaken something in you.

A sound you did not know you had.
A depth you did not know existed.
A weapon you did not know worked.

Because when you release a W.A.R. Cry, you do not just pray.

You shift realms.

Chapter 1
When Worship Becomes A Weapon

There is a dimension of worship many have not yet accessed.

It is not convenient
It is not dependent on music
It does not wait for everything to be right.

This kind of worship is a weapon.

Worship Is Not Just Expression. It Is Strategy.

Many view worship as emotional.

Worship is intentional.

It is a spiritual strategy designed by God to shift atmospheres, silence the enemy, and bring heaven into earthly situations.

When you understand worship, you stop waiting for the right moment and start using it in the middle of the battle.

Worship was never reserved for comfort.

It was designed for conflict.

The Battle You See Is Not Where It Started

Before anything manifests naturally, it begins spiritually.

The frustration you feel
The resistance you encounter
The heaviness you cannot explain.

These are rooted in the spirit.

If the battle started in the spirit, the victory must be won there.

Worship is how you fight where the battle actually is.

When Worship Confuses the Enemy

2 Chronicles 20:22
"And when they began to sing and to praise, the Lord set ambushments against the children of Ammon, Moab, and mount Seir; and they were smitten."

They worshipped, and God fought.

Biblical Example: Jehoshaphat's Strategy

Jehoshaphat received devastating news. A vast army was coming against him.

Instead of responding in fear, he sought the Lord.

God instructed him to send worshippers ahead of the army.

2 Chronicles 20:21
"He appointed singers unto the Lord… and as they went out before the army…"

The worshippers went first.

As they praised, God caused confusion among the enemy. They turned on each other, and the battle was won before Judah ever lifted a sword.

When worship goes first, victory follows.

Biblical Example: Paul and Silas

Acts 16:25–26
"At midnight Paul and Silas prayed, and sang praises unto God… and suddenly there was a great earthquake…"

Paul and Silas were beaten, chained, and imprisoned.

Not comfortable.
Not favorable.
Not supported.

Yet at midnight, the darkest hour, they chose worship.

Not silent prayer alone, but intentional praise.

And suddenly:

The prison shook.
Chains broke.
Doors opened.

Worship did not just shift their emotions.

It shifted their environment.

Worship does not just fight battles.

It breaks limitations.

A Practical Example

You receive a report that tries to steal your peace.

Your natural response may be panic or overthinking.

But instead, you pause and worship:

God, I thank You.
You are still in control.
You are still faithful.

Nothing changes immediately in the natural.

But something shifts within.

Peace replaces anxiety.
Faith rises above fear.
Clarity replaces confusion.

You just used worship as a weapon.

You Cannot Worship and Worry at the Same Time

Worship magnifies God.
Worry magnifies the problem.

What you magnify becomes greater in your life.

Choose worship.

Worship Is a Sound the Enemy Cannot Fight

True worship comes from your spirit.

When your spirit releases a sound unto God, it disrupts every assignment sent against you.

Many Worship. Few Surrender.

Worship is not just singing.

It is surrender.

Until your heart bows, your worship has not fully risen.

Worship Requires Surrender

John 4:24
"God is Spirit, and those who worship Him must worship in spirit and in truth."

Real worship says:

Even if nothing changes, You are still God.

Worship in the Middle of the Battle

Worship in pain carries weight.

It is rooted in revelation, not circumstance.

Worship Activates Heaven

Worship invites God into your situation.

And when God steps in, everything must respond.

Your First Weapon in Your W.A.R. Cry

Before the cry comes worship.

Worship positions your heart.
Worship aligns your spirit.
Worship invites God into your battle.

Reflection

Take a moment to examine your posture.

Do I only worship when things are going well?
What is my first response in pressure—worry or worship?
Have I been singing, or have I surrendered?
What situation in my life requires worship instead of control?

Write your response:

Activation: Releasing Worship as a Weapon

Identify one battle you are currently facing.

Lift your hands and thank God, not for the outcome, but for who He is.

Declare His nature over your situation:

Healer.
Provider.
Deliverer.

Remain in that posture until you feel a shift.

This is how you train your spirit to respond with worship instead of worry.

Declaration

I will not wait for perfect conditions to worship.
I will worship in the middle of the battle.

My worship is a weapon.
As I worship, God fights for me.

Prayer

Father,

Teach me how to worship beyond my feelings.

Help me trust You in every situation.

When I feel overwhelmed, remind me that worship is my weapon.

Let my worship shift every atmosphere around me.

Fight every battle I cannot see.

In Jesus' name,
Amen.

Chapter 2
The Power Of Adoration

Intimacy Before Intervention

There is a level of relationship with God that goes beyond asking.

It goes beyond requests.
It goes beyond needs.
It goes beyond desperation.

It is called adoration.

Adoration is not about what God can do for you.
It is about who God is to you.

Many believers have learned how to pray.

Few have learned how to sit.

Adoration Is Love Without Agenda

There was a time when my prayers were filled with requests.

I knew how to ask.
I knew how to cry out.
I knew how to go before God when I needed something.

But I had not yet learned how to love Him without needing anything in return.

When you have lived through real life, real pain, and real battles, you often approach God from a place of survival.

But God does not just want your survival prayers.

He wants your surrendered heart.

Adoration removes the agenda.

It says:

God, even if You do not do another thing for me, You have already done enough.

From Brokenness to Intimacy

God did not just change my circumstances.

He changed me.

Not just outwardly, but deep within.

There was a version of me that reacted quickly, carried wounds, and responded from pain.

But God began to cleanse me in a way that left no residue.

In that process, I learned something:

Transformation does not happen in noise.

It happens in presence.

There were moments when I had nothing to say.

No requests.
No long prayers.

Just tears.

And those tears became my adoration.

There were times I sat in awe of His grace, His mercy, and His glory, realizing I should not be where I am today.

Adoration shifts you from asking to appreciating.

Adoration Builds Relationship

You cannot carry real authority without real intimacy.

God took me deeper, not just in ministry, but in relationship.

Before the platform, there was presence.
Before the preaching, there was prayer.
Before doors opened, there were private moments where it was just me and God.

Those moments built something in me that people could not see, but they could feel.

What is built in private will always manifest in public.

Biblical Example: Mary and Martha

Luke 10:38–42

Martha was busy serving.
Mary was sitting.

Martha was distracted.
Mary was devoted.

Jesus said Mary chose the better part.

Mary understood something many miss:

Being with Jesus is more important than doing for Him.

There was a season I could have been consumed with building, working, and doing ministry.

But God slowed me down.

He was not just building a ministry.

He was building me.

Adoration Attracts the Presence of God

Psalm 63:3
"Because thy lovingkindness is better than life, my lips shall praise thee."

There were seasons I had to remind myself:

God, You are better than anything I am believing You for.

Better than the doors.
Better than the opportunities.
Better than the expansion.

If you are not careful, you will begin to chase what God can do and forget to pursue who He is.

Adoration keeps your heart aligned.

Biblical Example: The Woman with the Alabaster Box

Luke 7:37–38

She came broken.
She came vulnerable.
She came unashamed.

And she poured everything out at His feet.

That story became personal to me.

Because I understand what it means to pour out.

To give God your pain.
Your past.
Your tears.
Your everything.

People may not understand your worship when they do not know your story.

They may misjudge your posture.

But they do not know the cost of your oil.

They do not know what it took for you to get free.

They do not know what you had to surrender to become who you are today.

Adoration is costly.

But it is worth it.

Adoration Will Cost You

It will cost you your pride.
It will cost you your image.
It will cost you the need to be understood.

There were times I chose silence instead of reacting.

Times I chose surrender instead of defending myself.

Not because I was weak.

Because I understood the value of what God was doing in me.

The oil on my life is too valuable to waste on unnecessary battles.

A Practical Example

There are moments where I intentionally shift my posture.

Not to ask.
Not to perform.

But simply to adore.

God, I love You.
You have kept me.
You have covered me.
You have carried me.

And in those moments, His presence becomes real.

Peace fills the room.
Clarity settles my mind.
Strength fills my spirit.

Nothing may change outwardly.

But everything shifts inwardly.

Adoration Shifts Your Focus

Adoration takes your eyes off your situation and places them on your Savior.

From pressure to presence.
From stress to surrender.
From worry to worship.

Adoration Prepares You for Authority

Before God trusts you with more, He develops you in private.

Adoration teaches you how to stay low.

So when God lifts you, you do not lose your posture.

Adoration Is the Foundation of Your W.A.R. Cry

Worship positions you.
Adoration deepens you.

It moves you from surface-level faith into real relationship.

Because a true W.A.R. Cry is not just loud.

It is rooted in intimacy.

Reflection

Do I spend more time asking than adoring?
Has my relationship with God become transactional?
What has God brought me through that I need to thank Him for?
Where is God calling me deeper?

Write your response:

Activation: Entering Into Adoration

Set aside intentional time with God.

Do not ask for anything.

Begin to love Him:

Father, I adore You.
You are faithful.
You are holy.
You are everything to me.

Stay there.

Let your heart connect.
Let your spirit rest.

This is where transformation happens.

Declaration

I will love God beyond what He does for me.
I will pursue His presence above all things.
I will grow in intimacy and not just activity.

My relationship with God is my foundation.

Prayer

Father,

Teach me how to adore You.

Remove every mindset that has made my relationship with You about performance or need.

Draw me into deeper intimacy with You.

Let my love for You be pure, consistent, and unwavering.

And as I grow closer to You, let my life reflect Your glory.

In Jesus' name,
Amen.

Chapter 3
When The Battle Feels Personal

Not every battle feels the same.

Some are external.
Some are visible.
Some you can explain.

Then there are battles that feel personal.

The kind that touches your heart.
The kind that hits your emotions.
The kind that makes you question what you thought you understood.

These battles do not just challenge your strength.

They challenge your identity.

When It Hits Close to Home

There are moments when the warfare does not come from strangers.

It comes from places you did not expect.

From people you loved.
From people you helped.
From people you opened doors for.

If you are not careful, you will take it personally.

You will internalize what was never meant to define you.

When something feels personal, it is easy to ask:

God, why me?
Why did this happen this way?
Why did they treat me like this?

But you must understand this:

Not everything that feels personal is about you.

The Enemy Targets What Carries Oil

The attack is not random.

It is strategic.

The enemy does not waste time on what is not a threat.

He targets what carries purpose.
He targets what carries weight.
He targets what carries oil.

When there is something valuable on your life, the attack will often come through people.

Misunderstanding.
Rejection.
Opposition.

Not because you are wrong.

Because you are anointed.

My Test: Learning Not to Take It Personally

There were moments in my journey where I had to learn this in real time.

Moments where I gave my heart, served with sincerity, and showed up with purity, yet still faced misunderstanding.

Moments where I had to watch people walk away.

Not because of conflict.

Because of calling.

If I am honest, it could have hurt me in a way that shut me down.

It could have made me question myself.
It could have made me hard.
It could have made me guarded.

But God would not allow me to stay there.

What He was building in me was greater than what I was feeling around me.

Biblical Example: David and Saul

1 Samuel 18:8–9

David served Saul faithfully.

He honored him.
He fought for him.
He protected his kingdom.

But Saul became jealous.

The same David who was celebrated became targeted.

The attack was not because David did something wrong.

It was because of what was on his life.

Saul saw the favor.
Saul saw the oil.
Saul saw the future.

And instead of celebrating it, he fought it.

This is what happens when the battle feels personal.

You Cannot Fight Spiritual Battles with Emotional Reactions

When something feels personal, your flesh wants to respond.

To defend.
To explain.

To prove.
To correct.

But not every battle requires your voice.

Some battles require your silence.

If you respond in your flesh, you step out of position.

And when you step out of position, you delay what God is doing.

God Will Use It to Develop You

Every personal battle carries purpose.

It exposes what is in you.
It refines your character.
It strengthens your spirit.

There were moments I had to choose:

Will I react or will I grow?
Will I defend myself or trust God to handle it?

Every time I chose surrender over reaction, something in me became stronger.

When People Misjudge You

One of the hardest things to endure is being misunderstood.

When people assume wrong.
When they create narratives.
When they judge without knowing your heart.

I learned something powerful:

People can only misjudge what they do not understand.

And everyone is not assigned to understand you.

Instead of explaining yourself to everyone, stay aligned with God.

His validation is greater than public opinion.

A Practical Example: Choosing Posture Over Reaction

There were times I could have responded.

Times I could have spoken.
Times I could have corrected people.

But I chose posture.

I stepped back.
I prayed.
I surrendered.

Not because I had nothing to say.

Because I understood what was at stake.

The oil on my life is too valuable to waste on unnecessary battles.

God Is Fighting Battles You Cannot See

While you are trying to understand what is happening, God is already working.

He is shifting people.
He is closing doors.
He is revealing hearts.
He is aligning purpose.

What feels like loss is often protection.

What feels like rejection is often redirection.

When the Battle Feels Personal, Go Back to Worship

This is where everything connects.

When it feels personal, worship.
When it hurts, worship.
When you do not understand, worship.

Worship keeps your heart clean.

And a clean heart keeps you aligned with God.

Your W.A.R. Cry in Personal Battles

This is where your W.A.R. Cry deepens.

Worship keeps you grounded.
Adoration keeps you connected.
Reverence keeps you aligned.

And your cry becomes:

God, I trust You with what I do not understand.

Reflection

What situation have I taken personally that I need to release?
Have I allowed people's actions to affect my identity?
Am I reacting in my flesh or responding in my spirit?
What is God developing in me through this season?

Write your response:

Activation: Releasing Personal Battles to God

Identify what has hurt or offended you.

Bring it before God honestly.

Release the need to defend yourself.

Choose worship instead of reaction.

Say:

God, I give this to You. I trust You to handle what I cannot.

Declaration

I will not take what is spiritual personally.
I will not allow people to define me.
I will remain aligned with God in every situation.

My oil is too valuable to waste on unnecessary battles.

Prayer

Father,

Heal every place in me that has been hurt by what felt personal.

Give me the wisdom to discern what is spiritual and not internalize what was never meant to define me.

Help me respond in the spirit and not in my flesh.

Strengthen my heart, guard my mind, and keep me aligned with You.

Remind me in every battle that You are fighting for me.

In Jesus' name,
Amen.

Chapter 4
When The Battle Feels Too Heavy

There are battles that challenge you.

And there are battles that feel like they are trying to crush you.

The kind of weight that does not just sit on your shoulders.
It presses on your mind.
It drains your strength.
It exhausts your spirit.

These are the moments when you are not asking, How do I win?

You are asking, How do I keep going?

When Strength Feels Drained

There are seasons where you feel strong.

Focused.
Confident.
Grounded.

Then there are seasons where everything feels heavy.

You are still praying, but you feel tired.
You are still showing up, but it takes more effort.
You are still believing, but the weight is real.

Many people do not talk about this part.

We are taught how to be strong.

But we are not always taught how to be sustained.

You Can Be Anointed and Still Feel Heavy

Being called does not cancel pressure.

Being anointed does not eliminate weight.

Being chosen does not remove the process.

There were moments in my journey where I carried responsibility, vision, and expectation all at once.

Building.
Leading.
Pouring.
Showing up for others.

And while people saw strength, there were moments I felt the weight.

Moments where I had to go back to God and say:

Lord, I need You to carry what I cannot.

Biblical Example: Elijah Under the Juniper Tree

1 Kings 19:4

Elijah had just experienced a major victory.

Fire fell from heaven.
Prophets were defeated.
God moved powerfully.

But right after that victory, he found himself overwhelmed.

Tired.
Afraid.
Emotionally drained.

He sat under a tree and said:

It is enough.

This matters.

It shows that even powerful, anointed people can have moments where it feels too heavy.

God Does Not Rebuke Your Weakness

When Elijah said, It is enough, God did not rebuke him.

God responded.

He allowed him to rest.
He sent provision.
He restored his strength.

God does not expect you to carry everything alone.

He responds to your honesty.

My Reality: Learning to Lay It Down

There were moments where I had to be honest with God.

Not strong.
Not composed.
Not put together.

Just honest.

God, this is heavy.

When you are building, leading, and carrying vision, there is a weight that comes with it.

People see the outcome, but they do not always see the pressure.

I had to learn:

I cannot carry what belongs to God.

You Were Never Meant to Carry It All

Matthew 11:28
"Come unto me, all ye that labour and are heavy laden, and I will give you rest."

God did not say figure it out.

He said come to Me.

Rest is not found in removing the responsibility.

It is found in releasing the weight.

Heavy Does Not Mean You Are Failing

Sometimes we think if it feels heavy, something is wrong.

But heavy does not mean failure.

Heavy can mean:

You are growing.
You are stretching.
You are carrying something significant.

The weight is often an indication that what is on your life matters.

A Practical Example: Releasing the Weight

There are moments where I intentionally stop.

Not to quit, but to reset.

I go before God and say:

Father, I give You everything that is trying to weigh me down.
The pressure.
The responsibility.
The expectations.

Then I sit in His presence.

No performance.
No pressure.

Just release.

And every time, something shifts.

Peace replaces pressure.

Strength replaces exhaustion.
Clarity replaces overwhelm.

God Will Strengthen You in the Middle of It

Isaiah 40:29
"He giveth power to the faint; and to them that have no might he increaseth strength."

God may not remove the situation immediately.

But He will strengthen you in it.

He will sustain you through it.

He will carry you when you feel like you cannot carry yourself.

You Cannot Pour Out if You Are Empty

If you are constantly pouring into others but never allowing God to pour into you, you will become drained.

Eventually, you will feel the weight more than the grace.

I had to learn:

I cannot give what I do not have.

I cannot pour from an empty place.

So I made a decision to prioritize presence over pressure.

Because what fills me in private sustains me in public.

When the Battle Feels Too Heavy, Return to His Presence

This is where everything connects.

Worship lifts the weight.
Adoration restores your heart.

Reverence realigns your spirit.

And your cry becomes:

God, I cannot carry this, but I trust You to.

Your W.A.R. Cry in Heavy Seasons

This is not a loud cry.

This is a surrendered cry.

I release it.
I trust You.
I lean on You.

And in that place, God meets you.

Reflection

What am I carrying that I was never meant to carry alone?
Have I been honest with God about how I feel?
Am I resting in God or just pushing through pressure?
What do I need to release today?

Write your response:

Activation: Releasing the Weight

Take a moment and do this intentionally:

Name what feels heavy.
Speak it before God.
Release it mentally and spiritually.
Sit in His presence without rushing.

Say:

God, I give You what I cannot carry. Strengthen me where I feel weak.

Declaration

I will not carry what belongs to God.
I will release every burden that weighs me down.
God is my strength, and He is sustaining me.

I am not overwhelmed. I am supported by God.

Prayer

Father,

You see every weight I carry.
You know every pressure I feel.

Teach me how to release what I was never meant to hold alone.

Strengthen me in my weak moments.
Restore me in my tired places.
Sustain me in every season.

Remind me that I am never carrying this by myself.

In Jesus' name,
Amen.

Chapter 5
The Power Of Bending In Prayer

Surrender That Produces Strength

There is a posture in the spirit many avoid.

Yet it is the very place where power is released.

It is called bending.

Bending is not weakness.
Bending is not defeat.
Bending is not giving up.

Bending is surrender.

And in the Kingdom of God, surrender is not loss.

It is access.

Bending Is a Posture, Not Just a Position

Many know how to pray.

Few understand posture.

You can say the right words and still carry the wrong heart.

Bending is not just about your knees.

It is about your spirit.

Your will bows.
Your emotions bow.
Your understanding bows.

And you say:

God, not my will, but Yours.

My Journey: Learning to Bend Without Breaking

There were moments I had to decide:

Would I break under pressure, or bend in prayer?

Life will present situations you cannot control.

Moments that stretch you.
Moments that challenge you.
Moments that try to pull a reaction out of you.

But God taught me something:

If you bend before Me, you will not break in life.

There were times I had to go low.

Not before people.

Before God.

I had to surrender my emotions.
Surrender my response.
Surrender my need to understand everything.

And in that place of bending, God strengthened me.

Biblical Example: Jesus in Gethsemane

Luke 22:41–42
"And he kneeled down, and prayed… saying, Father, if thou be willing, remove this cup from me: nevertheless not my will, but thine, be done."

Jesus felt the weight.

He knew the cost.

He understood what was coming.

And He bent.

He did not resist the will of God.

He surrendered to it.

That moment of bending produced the strength He needed to endure the cross.

Bending Produces Strength, Not Weakness

In the natural, bending can look like losing.

In the spirit, bending builds strength.

Because when you bend:

You release control.
You receive grace.
You activate heaven.

God does not strengthen the resistant.

He strengthens the surrendered.

We Resist What We Do Not Understand

Surrender is often hardest when things do not make sense.

When the outcome is unclear.
When the process is uncomfortable.

But bending says:

God, I trust You even when I do not understand You.

A Practical Example: Choosing Prayer Over Reaction

There were moments I could have reacted.

Moments I could have spoken.
Moments I could have defended myself.

But I chose to bend.

To go into prayer instead of conversation.
To surrender instead of react.

Not because I was weak.

Because I understood my strength was in God.

Every time I chose prayer over reaction, God handled what I could not.

Bending Breaks Pride

One of the greatest barriers to bending is pride.

Pride says:

I can handle this.
I got this.
I do not need help.

Bending says:

God, I need You.

Until you recognize your dependence on God, you will struggle to walk in His fullness.

Bending Aligns You with God's Will

When you bend, you come into alignment.

Your desires shift.
Your perspective changes.
Your decisions become clearer.

You are no longer operating from your will.

You are operating from His.

Bending Is Where Instructions Are Released

Some of the clearest direction I have ever received came in moments of surrender.

Not in noise.
Not in movement.
In stillness.
In prayer.
In bending.
When everything else is quiet, you can finally hear God.

When You Refuse to Bend, Pressure Increases

Pressure increases when surrender is delayed.

The longer you hold on, the heavier it becomes.

But the moment you release it to God, the weight lifts.

Not because the situation is gone.

Because you are no longer carrying it alone.

Your W.A.R. Cry in Bending

This is where your cry deepens.

Not loud.

Not emotional.

Surrendered.

God, I give You everything.
My will, my plans, my emotions—I lay them at Your feet.

And in that place, God meets you.

Reflection

What area of my life is God asking me to surrender?
Am I resisting what God is trying to do in me?
Have I been reacting instead of praying?
What would it look like to fully trust God in this season?
Write your response:

Activation: Bending in Prayer

Take intentional time to do this:

Find a quiet place.
Posture yourself in surrender, physically or spiritually.
Speak honestly to God.
Release control and say, Not my will, but Yours.

Stay there.

Let God minister to you.

Declaration

I choose to bend and not break.
I release control and trust God completely.
My strength comes from my surrender.
I am aligned with God's will for my life.

Prayer

Father,

Teach me how to bend before You.

Break every area of pride, resistance, and control in my life.

Help me trust You even when I do not understand.

Strengthen me in my surrender.
Guide me in Your will.
And let every moment of bending produce power in my life.

In Jesus' name,
Amen.

Chapter 6
Winning The Battle In Your Mind

Where the War Really Happens

Every battle does not start in your life.

It starts in your mind.

Before you quit, you thought about it.
Before you doubted, it crossed your mind.
Before fear showed up in your actions, it whispered in your thoughts.

The mind is the battlefield.

If the enemy can influence your thoughts, he can influence your life.

The Mind Is the Entry Point

The enemy does not always attack your situation first.

He attacks your thinking.

If he can get you to:

Think wrong
Believe wrong
Perceive wrong

You will eventually live wrong.

This is why your mind must be guarded.

Not Every Thought Is Yours

One of the greatest revelations you can receive is this:

Just because you thought it does not mean it came from you.

Some thoughts are suggestions.

Suggestions of fear.
Suggestions of doubt.
Suggestions of insecurity.

If you do not discern them, you will accept them.

My Journey: Learning to Silence the Noise

There were moments where my mind was filled with questions.

Thoughts that challenged what God said about me.

Are you really called to this?
Are you capable?
Are you doing enough?

If I am honest, those thoughts could have taken root.

But God taught me something:

You cannot entertain what you are supposed to cast down.

I had to learn how to reject thoughts that did not align with God.

Not emotionally.

Intentionally.

Biblical Principle: Casting Down Thoughts

2 Corinthians 10:5
"Casting down imaginations, and every high thing that exalteth itself against the knowledge of God…"

Notice the instruction:

Casting down.

Not ignoring.
Not entertaining.

Not negotiating.

Casting down.

Some thoughts are not meant to be managed.

They are meant to be rejected.

The Enemy Uses Your Mind Against You

If he cannot stop you physically, he will try to stop you mentally.

He will plant seeds like:

You are not enough.
This will not work.
You might as well give up.

If those thoughts are not confronted, they will grow.

Because what you entertain, you empower.

You Must Replace, Not Just Remove

You cannot just remove negative thoughts.

You must replace them.

An empty mind will always be filled again.

When a thought says:

You are not enough, respond:

I am who God says I am.

When a thought says:

You cannot handle this, respond:

God is my strength.

A Practical Example: Taking Authority Over Your Mind

There are moments now where I am intentional about what I allow.

If a thought does not align with God, I do not sit with it.

I speak against it.

God did not give me a spirit of fear.
I am called.
I am equipped.
I am covered.

Your voice has authority over your mind.

Your Mind Must Be Renewed Daily

Romans 12:2
"Be ye transformed by the renewing of your mind…"

This is not a one-time process.

It is daily.

Every day, you are exposed to something that can influence your thinking.

So every day, you must choose:

Truth over lies
Faith over fear
God's Word over your feelings

Your Thoughts Shape Your Reality

How you think determines how you live.

If you think defeated, you will live defeated.
If you think fearful, you will live restricted.
If you think aligned with God, you will walk in authority.

Guarding Your Mind Is Your Responsibility

God gives you the power.

But you must do the work.

Be mindful of what you listen to.
Be mindful of what you watch.
Be mindful of who you allow to speak into your life.

Everything that enters your mind plants a seed.

When the Battle Is in Your Mind, Return to Truth

This is where your W.A.R. Cry becomes strategic.

Worship silences fear.
Adoration centers your heart.
Reverence reminds you who God is.

And your cry becomes:

God, align my thoughts with Your truth.

You Win in Your Mind First

Victory does not start in your hands.

It starts in your mind.

Once your mind is aligned, your life will follow.

Reflection

What thoughts have I been entertaining that do not align with God?
Have I been accepting lies as truth?
What areas of my mind need to be renewed?
What do I need to replace with God's Word?

Write your response:

Activation: Taking Authority Over Your Mind

Identify one negative or limiting thought.

Write what God says about that area.

Speak that truth out loud daily.

Refuse to entertain anything that contradicts it.

Declaration

I have authority over my thoughts.
I reject every lie and embrace God's truth.
My mind is renewed, and my life is aligned.

I will think what God says about me.

Prayer

Father,

Renew my mind.

Help me recognize and reject every thought that does not align with
Your truth.

Strengthen me to walk in discipline and authority over my thinking.

Fill my mind with peace, clarity, and truth.

As my mind is transformed, let my life reflect Your power.

In Jesus' name,
Amen.

Chapter 7
Standing Strong In The Middle
Of The Battle

The Power of Not Quitting

There is a moment in every battle where the real fight is not about starting.

It is about staying.

Starting is easy when you are excited.
Starting is easy when you feel called.
Starting is easy when the vision is clear.

But staying requires strength.

The Battle Is Not Always About Defeat

Not every battle is meant to take you out.

Some are designed to wear you out.

To make you tired.
To make you question.
To make you consider walking away.

If the enemy cannot destroy you, he will try to exhaust you.

When Quitting Feels Like an Option

There are moments when quitting will feel reasonable.

Stepping back feels easier.
Letting go feels justified.
Walking away feels like relief.

But just because it feels easier does not mean it is right.

My Journey: Choosing to Stay

There were moments where it would have been easier to step back.

Moments where the weight, the responsibility, and the pressure could have made me reconsider everything.

Leading.
Building.
Pouring into others.

At times, it felt like I was giving more than I was receiving.

But God reminded me:

You are not called to convenience.

You are called to commitment.

In those moments, I had to decide:

Will I stay planted, or will I move based on how I feel?

Biblical Example: Jesus in the Wilderness

Matthew 4:1–11

Jesus was led into the wilderness.

He was tempted.
He was tested.
He was challenged.

The enemy presented Him with options:

Take the easy way.
Prove yourself.
Skip the process.

But Jesus stood.

He did not move based on pressure.
He did not respond out of emotion.

He remained grounded in the Word.

Standing Requires You to Be Rooted

If you are not rooted, you will be easily moved.

By people.
By emotions.
By situations.

But when you are rooted in God, you may feel pressure, but you will not be shaken.

You Do Not Have to Feel Strong to Stand Strong

Strength is not always a feeling.

Sometimes it is a decision.

A decision to keep showing up.
A decision to keep believing.
A decision to keep trusting God when it is not easy.

A Practical Example: Showing Up Anyway

There will be moments when you do not feel like it.

You may not feel motivated.
You may not feel energized.
You may not feel encouraged.

But you show up anyway.

You pray anyway.
You worship anyway.
You stay committed anyway.

Consistency builds strength.

Do Not Grow Weary

Galatians 6:9
"Let us not be weary in well doing: for in due season we shall reap, if we faint not."

The promise is connected to your ability to stay.

If we faint not.

Your breakthrough is not just about what you do.

It is about whether you remain.

Endurance Produces Maturity

James 1:3–4
"The trying of your faith worketh patience…"

Patience is not passive.

It is developed through pressure.

Every time you choose to stay when it is hard, you are becoming stronger.

More stable.
More grounded.
More mature.

When You Feel Like Giving Up, Go Back to Why You Started

There were moments I had to remind myself:

Why did God call me to this?
What did God show me?
What has God already brought me through?

When you reconnect with purpose, you regain strength.

God Is Sustaining You

There will be moments you feel like you are barely holding on.

But the truth is:

God is holding you.

Even when you feel weak, you are sustained.
Even when you feel tired, you are supported.
Even when you feel like stopping, God is strengthening you.

Your W.A.R. Cry in the Middle of the Battle

This is not a cry of panic.

This is a cry of perseverance.

God, I will not quit.
God, I trust You through this.
God, I will remain.

Worship keeps you anchored.
Adoration keeps you connected.
Reverence keeps you aligned.

And your cry becomes strength.

Reflection

Where have I been tempted to quit?
What has God called me to that I need to stay committed to?
Am I making decisions based on feelings or faith?
What is God strengthening in me through this season?

Write your response:

Activation: Strength to Stay

Identify the area where you feel like quitting.

Speak God's promises over that area.

Commit to showing up consistently.

Ask God for strength daily.

Say:

God, give me the strength to stay where You have called me.

Declaration

I will not quit.
I will remain planted and committed.
I am strengthened by God in every season.

What God started in me, He will complete.

Prayer

Father,

Give me the strength to stand in the middle of the battle.

When I feel tired, renew me.
When I feel weak, strengthen me.
When I feel like quitting, remind me of my purpose.

Help me remain rooted, consistent, and faithful.

And in every season, let me stand firm in You.

In Jesus' name,
Amen.

Chapter 8
The Victory After The Battle

When What You Survived Becomes Your Strength

Every battle has an end.

Every storm has a breaking point.
Every season has a transition.

There comes a moment when what tried to take you out can no longer hold you.

That moment is victory.

Victory Does Not Always Look Like You Expected

We often expect victory to be loud.

Celebration.
Applause.
Immediate turnaround.

But real victory is often quiet.

It looks like peace where there used to be anxiety.
It looks like strength where there used to be weakness.
It looks like clarity where there used to be confusion.

Victory is not always what changed around you.

Sometimes it is what changed within you.

My Reality: Becoming What I Survived

There are things I have walked through that could have broken me.

Moments that could have changed how I love, how I trust, and how I show up.

But instead of breaking me, God used it to build me.

I did not just survive it.

I became stronger because of it.

That is victory.

Not just getting through.

Becoming better.

Biblical Example: Joseph's Journey

Genesis 50:20
"What you meant for evil… God meant for good."

Joseph was betrayed by his brothers.
Sold into slavery.
Falsely accused.
Forgotten in prison.

His story was filled with battles.

Yet in the end, he saw purpose.

That is victory.

Not that the process was easy.

That the outcome was purposeful.

Victory Gives You Perspective

When you come out of a battle, you see differently.

Things that once mattered do not matter the same way.
Things that once shook you no longer move you.

Your perspective shifts.

You realize God was with you the entire time.

Do Not Lose the Lesson After the Battle

One of the biggest mistakes people make is surviving the battle but forgetting the lesson.

Every battle teaches you something.

About God.
About yourself.
About your strength.

If you do not retain the lesson, you may repeat the cycle.

Victory Requires Stewardship

Making it through is not the end.

Growth must continue.

Victory must be maintained.

Through discipline.
Through prayer.
Through consistency.

What God brings you into, you must learn how to steward.

A Practical Example: Walking in Victory Daily

There are moments now where I recognize:

I am not who I used to be.

I do not respond the same.
I do not react the same.
I do not think the same.

That is victory.

Victory is not just external success.

It is internal transformation.

Your Testimony Is Someone Else's Breakthrough

What you went through is not just for you.

It is for someone else.

Someone who is in the place you used to be.
Someone who needs to know it is possible to come out.

Your life becomes evidence.

God restores.
God heals.
God delivers.

Victory Is Not the End

It Is a New Beginning

After the battle comes responsibility.

You now carry more wisdom, more strength, and more understanding.

God will use what you went through to help someone else get through.

Stay Humble in Victory

Victory should never make you prideful.

It should make you grateful.

Everything you made it through, God brought you through.

When you remember that, you stay grounded.

Your W.A.R. Cry After the Battle

This is a cry of gratitude.

God, You did it.

God, You kept me.
God, You sustained me.

Worship becomes thanksgiving.
Adoration becomes appreciation.
Reverence becomes honor.

And your cry becomes:

God, I will never forget what You brought me through.

Reflection

What has God brought me through that I need to acknowledge?
What lessons did I learn in my last battle?
How has God changed me through my experiences?
How can I use my testimony to help someone else?

Write your response:

Activation: Walking in Victory

Reflect on a battle God has already brought you through.

Write down what you learned.

Thank God intentionally for bringing you out.

Share your testimony with someone who needs encouragement.

Declaration

I walk in victory.
I am stronger because of what I survived.
God has brought me through, and I will not forget it.

My life is a testimony of His power.

Prayer

Father,

Thank You for every battle You have brought me through.

Thank You for sustaining me, strengthening me, and keeping me.

Help me never forget what You have done.

Teach me how to walk in victory with humility, wisdom, and gratitude.

Use my life as a testimony to encourage and uplift others.

In Jesus' name,
Amen.

Chapter 9
Living A Life That Bends Before God

A Lifestyle of Surrender, Not Just a Moment

Bending is not meant to be a one-time response.

It is meant to be a lifestyle.

Many know how to surrender in a moment.

Few know how to stay surrendered daily.

It is easy to bend when you are desperate.
It is easy to bend when you need God to move.
It is easy to bend when the pressure is high.

But can you bend when things are going well?

Can you stay surrendered when there is no crisis?

That is where maturity is revealed.

Surrender Is Not Seasonal. It Is Daily

A life that bends before God is not built in emergencies.

It is built in consistency.

Daily surrender.
Daily alignment.
Daily choosing God over your own will.

If you only go to God when things are wrong, you will struggle to remain with Him when things are right.

My Journey: From Moments to Lifestyle

There was a time when my surrender was situational.

I went deeper when I needed something.
Prayed harder when things got heavy.
Sought God more when pressure increased.

But God shifted me.

From moment-based surrender to lifestyle surrender.

Where I began to include Him in everything.

Not just decisions, but daily living.
Not just battles, but blessings.

God Desires Consistency, Not Just Crisis

God is not just looking for you in difficult times.

He desires relationship in every season.

Morning.
Midday.
Night.

In quiet moments.
In busy moments.
In successful moments.

Real relationship is not based on need.

It is built on connection.

Biblical Example: Daniel's Consistency

Daniel 6:10
"He kneeled upon his knees three times a day, and prayed…"

Daniel did not wait for trouble to pray.

Prayer was his lifestyle.

So when pressure came, he did not have to develop a prayer life.

He already had one.

That is the power of consistency.

What You Build Daily Will Sustain You Spiritually

If you only build your spiritual life occasionally, you will struggle when real battles come.

But when you build daily:

Through prayer
Through worship
Through time with God

You become spiritually strong.

When life hits, you are already equipped.

A Life That Bends Is a Life That Listens

When you live surrendered, you become sensitive to God.

You begin to discern His voice.
Recognize His leading.
Respond quickly to His instruction.

Because your heart is already postured toward Him.

Surrender in the Small Things

Surrender is not just for major decisions.

It is found in the small things.

Your attitude.
Your response.

Your words.
Your choices.

Every day presents an opportunity:

Follow your flesh or follow God.

Every time you choose God, you are bending.

A Practical Example: Daily Alignment

There are moments now where I pause.

Before I respond.
Before I decide.
Before I move.

God, what are You saying?
God, how should I handle this?
God, align me with Your will.

I no longer want to move without Him.

That is what a surrendered life looks like.

Surrender Protects You

When you live a life that bends before God, you avoid unnecessary battles.

God will:

Redirect you.
Restrain you.
Reveal things to you.

Things you would not have seen on your own.

Surrender is protection.

You Cannot Live Two Ways

You cannot be surrendered and stubborn at the same time.

You cannot follow God and follow your flesh.

A decision must be made.

Who is leading your life?

Whatever leads you will shape your future.

Your W.A.R. Cry as a Lifestyle

At this level, your cry is no longer occasional.

It is consistent.

Worship becomes your daily posture.
Adoration becomes your natural expression.
Reverence becomes your foundation.

Your life becomes the cry.

Reflection

Is my relationship with God consistent or conditional?
Do I only seek God in difficult moments?
What areas of my life do I need to surrender daily?
How can I become more intentional about including God in my
everyday life?

Write your response:

Activation: Building a Lifestyle of Surrender

Set a daily time to spend with God.

Include God in your decisions throughout the day.

Pause before reacting and ask for direction.

Stay consistent, even when you do not feel like it.

Declaration

I live a life surrendered to God.
I choose Him daily, not just in difficult moments.
My life is aligned with His will.

I will walk in consistency and obedience.

Prayer

Father,

Teach me how to live a life fully surrendered to You.

Not just in moments of need, but in every area of my life.

Help me to be consistent, disciplined, and aligned with Your will.

Guide my decisions, shape my thoughts, and direct my steps.

Let my life reflect a daily posture of surrender before You.

In Jesus' name,
Amen.

Chapter 10
Releasing your W.A.R. Cry

The Sound That Shifts Everything

You have learned what it means to worship.
You have learned how to adore.
You have learned how to reverence God.

Now it is time to release it.

Because everything you have learned was not just for understanding.

It was for activation.

Your Sound Has Power

There is a sound inside of you.

Not borrowed.
Not copied.
Not performed.

It is personal.

It has been shaped by your experiences.
Refined through your battles.
Strengthened through your surrender.

And when you release it, it carries weight.

Because it is real.

You Cannot Stay Silent Anymore

Silence is no longer an option.

Not after what you have survived.
Not after what God has brought you through.

Not after what He has revealed to you.

There is a sound that must come out of you.

A sound of authority.
A sound of surrender.
A sound of victory.

Your W.A.R. Cry.

This Is Not About Volume—It Is About Depth

Your cry is not about how loud you are.

It is about how deep you are.

Because a real W.A.R. Cry does not come from your mouth alone.

It comes from your spirit.

It is where worship, adoration, and reverence come together and create a sound that heaven responds to.

Biblical Example: Blind Bartimaeus

Mark 10:46–52

Bartimaeus cried out.

Jesus, Son of David, have mercy on me.

People tried to silence him.

Told him to be quiet.
Told him to sit down.
Told him to stay in his place.

But he cried louder.

Because he understood something:

What I need is on the other side of my sound.

And when Jesus heard him, He stopped.

That is the power of a cry that comes from desperation and faith.

Your Cry Will Interrupt What Was Ignoring You

There are things that have not responded to your silence.

Situations that have not shifted.
Battles that have not moved.

But when your cry is released, it creates interruption.

Heaven responds.
Atmospheres shift.
Chains break.

Not because of volume.

Because of alignment.

You Have Been Prepared for This Moment

Everything you have gone through has prepared you for this.

Every battle.
Every test.
Every season.

It was building your sound.

So when you release it, it would carry authority.

You are not starting from scratch.

You are releasing what has already been developed.

A Practical Example: Releasing Your Cry

There are moments now where you do not hold back.

You do not overthink.

You do not filter.
You do not question.

You release.

God, I trust You.
God, I surrender.
God, I worship You.
God, I give You everything.

And as you release it, something shifts.

Not just around you.

Within you.

Your W.A.R. Cry Is a Weapon

Worship breaks resistance.
Adoration draws you closer.
Reverence keeps you aligned.

Together, they form your W.A.R. Cry.

A sound that fights.
A sound that shifts.
A sound that breaks through.

This Is a Call to Activation

This is not the end.

This is the beginning.

Because now you know:

How to worship in the battle.
How to adore beyond need.
How to reverence God in every season.
How to bend and not break.
How to stand and not quit.

How to guard your mind.
How to carry victory.
How to live surrendered.

Now it is time to live it.

Activation: Release Your W.A.R. Cry

Take a moment right now.

Do not rush.

Do not overthink.

Position yourself.

Lift your hands if you can.

And begin to release:

Worship Him for who He is.
Adore Him without asking.
Reverence Him with your posture.

Then open your mouth and let your sound come out.

Not perfect.

Real.

Let your spirit speak.

Stay there.

Let it rise.

Let it build.

Let it break through.

Declaration

I will not remain silent.
I will release the sound God placed inside of me.
My worship is powerful.
My adoration is pure.
My reverence is aligned.

My W.A.R. Cry will shift atmospheres and break every battle.

Final Prayer

Father,

Thank You for everything You have revealed through this journey.

Thank You for strengthening me, teaching me, and drawing me closer to You.

Today, I make a decision.

I will not remain silent.

I will release my worship, my adoration, and my reverence unto You.

Let my W.A.R. Cry shift every atmosphere around me.

Break every chain.
Destroy every stronghold.
Move in every situation.

And from this day forward, let my life reflect a continuous sound of surrender, authority, and victory.

In Jesus' name,
Amen.

Final Word

There is a sound inside of you.

And now…

It is time to release it.

About the Author

Pastor Sherrell Attaway is a transformational leader, author, and prophetic voice called to awaken, equip, and position individuals to walk in spiritual authority. Her assignment is clear—to help people break cycles, confront what has been fighting them, and step fully into the life God has called them to live.

As the founder of **Rebuilding the Broken International Ministries**, she leads with a focus on deliverance, restoration, and real-life transformation. Her ministry goes beyond inspiration. It is about activation, alignment, and results.

She is also the founder of the nonprofit organization **"It Only Takes a Spark,"** an initiative designed to ignite hope, purpose, and change in individuals and communities.

Pastor Attaway is the visionary behind the podcast
"Casting Thy Cares on the Water: Release It,"
where individuals are led through a process of releasing burdens, confronting pain, and stepping into healing and freedom.

A **global and international speaker**, she carries a message that reaches beyond walls and borders, challenging people to rise, move, and respond to the call of God on their lives.

In addition to ministry, she is a **serial business owner**, demonstrating that faith and marketplace success can coexist. Through her leadership and coaching, she equips others to turn their passion into purpose-driven income while maintaining integrity and alignment with God.

Her Message

Pastor Sherrell Attaway does not just teach about warfare.

She teaches how to win.

Her message is rooted in truth.

Silence is no longer an option.
Brokenness is not your identity.
And what has been fighting you can be defeated.

Final Word

There is a sound inside of you.

And when you release it…

Everything that has been standing against you must respond.

Connect | Booking | Speaking

For speaking engagements, ministry invitations, or media inquiries:

Phone: (404) 410-6455

Email: PastorAttaway@gmail.com

NOW
BOOKING
2026
PASTOR SHERRELL ATTAWAY
PASTOR • PROPHETESS • REVIVALIST
BOOKING INFO:
PHONE: (404) 410-6455
EMAIL: PastorAttaway@gmail.com